ONE NIGHT ON BROADWAY HORST HAMANN

ONE NIGHT ON BROADWAY HORST HAMANN

SCHIRMER /MOSEL

WORTH STREET

▸ 06:07:38

▸ 06:07:39

▸ 06:07:40

▸ 06:07:41

▸ 06:07:42

THOMAS
STREET

▸ 06:09:07

▸ 06:09:08

▸ 06:09:09

WAY

DUANE STREET

▸ 06:10:21

▸ 06:10:22

▸ **06:10:23**

▸ 06:10:24

▸ 06:10:25

READE STREET

▸ 06:12:48

▸ 06:12:49

▸ 06:12:50

▸ 06:12:51

CHAMBERS STREET

▸ 06:13:11

▸ 06:13:12

▸ 06:13:13

▸ 06:13:14

▸ 06:13:15

WARREN STREET

- 06:19:31
- 06:19:32
- 06:19:33
- 06:19:34
- 06:19:35

MURRAY STREET

▸ 06:20:59

▸ 06:21:00

▸ 06:21:01

▸ 06:21:02

▸ 06:21:03

PARK PLACE

- 06:21:33
- 06:21:34
- 06:21:35
- 06:21:36
- 06:21:37

BARCLAY STREET

▸ 06:23:58
▸ 06:23:59
▸ 06:24:00
▸ 06:24:01
▸ 06:24:02

THE BRAVEST OF THE BRAVE
FDNY
9.11.01
THANK YOU FOR THE LIVES YOU SA
WWW.ARTAID.ORG

VESEY STREET

▸ 06:26:20

▸ 06:26:21

▸ 06:26:22

▸ 22:26:23

▸ 22:26:24

FULTON STREET

▸ 06:30:00
▸ 06:30:01
▸ 06:30:02
▸ 06:30:03
▸ 06:30:04
▸ 06:30:05

195 Broadway
HJ Kalikow & Co LLC
Owner Builder

▸ 06:43:13

▸ 06:43:14

▸ 06:43:15

▸ 06:43:16

▸ 06:43:17

COURTLANDT STREET / MAIDEN LANE

▸ 06:46:20

▸ 06:46:21

▸ 06:46:22

▸ 06:49:50

▸ 06:49:51

▸ 06:49:52

▸ 06:49:53

▸ 06:49:54

CEDAR STREET

▸ 06:50:47

▸ 06:50:48

▸ 06:50:49

▸ 06:50:50

▸ 06:50:51

▸ 06:51:28
▸ 06:51:29
▸ 06:51:30
▸ 06:51:31
▸ 06:51:32

PINE STREET

▸ 06:51:59

▸ 06:52:00

▸ 06:52:01

▸ 06:52:02

▸ 06:52:03

▸ 06:53:56
▸ 06:53:57
▸ 06:53:58
▸ 06:53:59
▸ 06:54:00

▶ 06:55:45

▶ 06:55:46

▶ 06:55:47

▶ 06:55:48

▶ 06:55:49

EXCHANGE ALLEY / EXCHANGE PLACE

- 07:03:43
- 07:03:44
- 07:03:45
- 07:03:46
- 07:03:47

MORRIS STREET

▸ 07:05:10

▸ 07:05:11

▸ 07:05:12

▸ 07:05:13

▸ 07:05:14

▸ 07:09:49

▸ 07:09:50

▸ 07:09:51

▸ 07:09:52

▸ 07:09:53

BOWLING GREEN

▸ 07:13:43

▸ 07:13:44

▸ 07:13:45

▸ 07:13:46

BATTERY PLACE

▸ 07:16:19
▸ 07:16:20
▸ 07:16:21
▸ 07:16:22
▸ 07:16:23

BATTERY PARK

▸ 07:27:17

▸ 07:27:18

▸ 07:27:19

▸ 07:27:20

"I found more poetry in New York that night than in any other place I traveled to."

– Horst Hamann

A Talk With Horst Hamann

by Katja Guttmann

Horst Hamann knows the metropolis New York is no dead pile of steel and stone, but a living "Goliath, embedded between the East and the Hudson River". In his coffee-table book *New York* (2001) he wrote, "He lies there, strapped down and connected by strings of bridges and tunnels, which provide him with daily sustenance – new dreams and illusions. Artificially kept alive by all those bending over him. Connected to the electrocardiogram of good and evil, of heaven and hell. He writhes, quivers and wheezes, sweats and moans. A bundle of energy constantly at risk of getting short-circuited. This giant warrior made of steel and glass, of marble and gold."

Not surprisingly, the German photographer uses the same metaphor for his project *One Night on Broadway*: "I wanted to feel the pulse of the city ..." On September 11, 2002, one year after the terror attacks shook "Goliath" to its core, Hamann set off to check on the city he has known for 23 years. He chose the aorta of the giant: Broadway. For the instrument to measure the blood pressure, Hamann selected the Digilux 1 by Leica. He also opted to shoot entirely by night on the anniversary. Call it a strictly personal challenge. Usually, Hamann uses only traditional cameras, like Linhof or Hasselblad, and he normally shoots during daylight. But his first experiments with night-time use of digital cameras convinced him otherwise.

And so he set out in the evening at 7:29. He started in Harlem with two assistants, Ax and Nate, at 125th Street. They finished the next morning at 7:27 in Battery Park on the Southern tip of Manhattan with a perfect view of the Statue of Liberty. The Mexican filmmaker Adolfo Doering recorded short conversations with people encountered along the way. They made it onto the CD *N.Y. Lounge: One Night on Broadway* (Black Flame 88162).

Why did you choose Broadway for this project?

Horst Hamann: I set out to feel the pulse of the city: How does New York feel one year after? I wanted to check New York's heartbeat. And I wanted to do it in one stretch, because the whole city is just too big. I chose Broadway, because it is the most representative street in New York, comparable to the Kudamm of Berlin or the Champs-Elysées of Paris. It's much better than hanging out only at Times Square, where you have all the tourists, or just being in Harlem, where your perception is different and, again, Soho would be entirely different than Tribeca. Even if you stroll down Fifth Avenue, your impressions can vary. Broadway is most exciting seen as a cross section. You have the entire spectrum of characters, architecture, pubs, people with cell phones, telephone booths, laundromats, delis, newsstands and night workers. Just everything.

While walking, what impressed you most?

HH: The entire atmosphere, especially the mixture of people, colors, the clutter of architecture and lights and life and energy and rhythm. As I said, it was like checking the pulse of a person. I didn't want to limit myself by merely snapping mugshots of the city, I wanted to feel the city physically. I usually hear and smell my pictures. New York is not just an optical experience, but simultaneously an acoustical experience, an olfactory experience, a haptic experience. Feeling the city, its vibrations, the subway grumbling underneath your feet, the odors mixing – it all fascinates me. Twelve hours on Broadway is an ideal example for such a short time. I was walking and sprinting and ducking down to get my pictures. And all around me were the tangle of languages, the theater, the honking. Those noises never annoy me, I love them. I miss it as soon as I leave the city. The conversations with people on the street were short trips into miscellaneous lifetimes. In the end, I had them all crammed in my head like pieces of a jigsaw puzzle. This night on Broadway was a megadose of vitamins. A New York injection. A prescription for therapy. I ought to do this every year from now on – other people run the marathon, I walk down Broadway.

What equipment did you take along?

HH: I took two Digilux 1's from Leica with me. I used 9 rechargeable batteries, as the cameras ran for 12 straight hours. I used 16 storage cards for a combined 2.3 gigabytes. While walking down Broadway, I even had to delete some of my pictures to make sure enough storage space remained. I also carried a laptop along, in case I ran out of power and had to download some of my material. Fortunately, I didn't have to. By the way, the most important piece of equipment is good shoes. I have been preaching for years to all my friends visiting New York. Choose comfortable footgear.

So you walked twelve hours straight, with virtually no break?

HH: We just had some coffee breaks. On a tour like that I can't eat anything, or I would collapse. I knew I had to walk for twelve consecutive hours. I had my mind set on it. I started at 7:29 in Harlem at 125th Street and finished the next morning in Battery Park at 7:27. The very last picture was corny, but rather symbolic: Two lovebirds are hugging, facing towards the Statue of Liberty. It was a wonderful morning, the sun was rising, we were as white as chalk, yet happy. Judging from the mental energy, we could have walked all the way back. Physically, however, we were exhausted.

How did someone like you, a crusader for traditional photography, end up using a digital camera for this project?

HH: Jimmy Breslin, columnist of the daily paper *Newsday* wrote a story entitled "A Smile Gone, But Where?" His son Kevin works as a movie director and is an old friend of mine and a real New Yorker. He faxed me his father's article and wanted to recreate the story as a movie. Seven years ago, I had worked together with Kevin on an educational movie about AIDS, which has been shown at Madison Square Garden. Since then he has kept pushing me about doing more film projects together. I kept telling him that I prefer still photography, but that I would reconsider for an exceptionally intriguing project. I liked his father's story very much, but the technical challenges of shooting at night horrified me. However, after several succesful tests with a digital video camera, I agreed. In November, we shot each night for one week, from dusk 'til dawn.

And while there, it hit me: It is unbelievable what digital video cameras are able to capture by night – I couldn't quite fathom it. The night shadows on the trees or gutters, which you usually don't notice, exhilarated. Though we were shooting on a rather boring block, 68th Street between Amsterdam and Broadway, next to the windowless sidewall of a huge cinema, you could see all detail, translated and enhanced through the camera. It was a revelation. Always a night owl, I had never been able to translate that into my work as a photographer. Until now. The next day I went to my photo store and bought my very first digital camera. They charged the battery for me and I started shooting right away.

How did the digital technology influence your work?

HH: While teaching photography workshops at the International Center of Photography (ICP) in New York I used to preach for analog photography. But I was indoctrinated. The results were downright mind-boggling, they really inspired me to do this Broadway project. From this time on, I kept taking pictures at night, digitally, no matter where I was, in Paris, New York or Berlin.

What's so different about digital photography?

HH: For this particular project the digital camera was an ideal tool to master the requirements. I can take hand-held shots – which complies with my usual technique. Traditional cameras don't allow you that: you normally have to expose each picture for minutes, using a tripod and cable release. People are gone by then, they are always in motion. I had already stopped using the tripod during my project *New York Vertical*, compensating by using a film with higher sensitivity. I realized I was being constrained by tripods. I must have freedom to move steadily, I have to be able to sneak around, to dance on the streets. If I had to arrange and adjust the tripod every few minutes, I would be missing so many great situations. Then after two pictures, I would lose interest.

The Digilux was perfect for that visual adventure. I compose right there on the display, I never use the viewfinder. At night, all the colors start mixing. You get color temperatures that are invisible to the naked eye: the cold neon light from the subway shafts, as well as the entire palette of warm colors, such as yellow and reds. The camera transforms into brush. Taking pictures becomes like painting or like catching the light.

Ein Gespräch mit Horst Hamann

Katja Guttmann

Für Horst Hamann ist die Weltmetropole New York kein toter Haufen aus Stahl und Steinen, sondern ein lebendiges Wesen, ein „Goliath, eingebettet zwischen East und Hudson River", wie er in seinem Bildband *New York* (2001) schreibt: „Angeschnallt und angestöpselt an zwei Handvoll Brücken und Tunnel, die ihn täglich mit frischem Blut und neuen Träumen und Illusionen versorgen, künstlich am Leben gehalten von all denen, die Tag und Nacht über ihn wachen, angeschlossen an das EKG, das Gut und Böse, Himmel und Hölle mißt. Er windet sich, zuckt, faucht, schwitzt und spuckt. Ein Energiepaket ständig vor dem Kurzschluß, ein gigantischer Krieger aus Stahl und Glas, aus Marmor und Gold."

Kein Wunder also, daß der deutsche Fotograf dasselbe Sinnbild für dieses Projekt benutzt: „Ich wollte den Puls der Stadt fühlen ..." Am 11. September 2002, genau ein Jahr, nachdem die Terroranschläge den „Goliath" in seinem Mark getroffen hatten, machte sich Hamann auf den Weg, um zu sehen, wie es seiner Stadt geht, die er seit 23 Jahren kennt. Er wählte dafür die Hauptschlagader des Molochs aus: den Broadway.

Als Instrument zur Pulsmessung diente Hamann die Leica Digilux 1. Als Zeitpunkt bestimmte er die zwölf Nachtstunden des Jahrestages. Beides war eine persönliche Herausforderung. Denn zum einen hatte er bis dahin nur analoge Kameras, wie die Linhof oder die Hasselblad, benutzt. Und zum anderen hauptsächlich bei Tageslicht im Freien gearbeitet. Aber erste Versuche mit digitalen Kameras überzeugten ihn.

Und so machte er sich am Abend um 19.29 Uhr auf den Weg. Er startete mit zwei Assistenten, Ax und Nate, an der 125th Street in Harlem und endete am nächsten Morgen um 7.27 Uhr an der Südspitze von Manhattan, im Battery Park mit Blick auf die Freiheitsstatue. Der mexikanische Filmemacher Adolfo Doering nahm kurze Gespräche mit den

Menschen auf, die sie unterwegs trafen. Daraus ist die CD *N.Y. Lounge: One Night on Broadway* entstanden (Black Flame 88162).

Warum haben Sie sich gerade den Broadway für Ihre Nachtaktion ausgesucht?

Horst Hamann: Ich wollte den Puls der Stadt fühlen: Wie geht es New York ein Jahr danach? Ich wollte den Gesundheitszustand von New York überprüfen. Und ich wollte es an einem Straßenzug ablesen, denn die ganze Stadt ist einfach zu groß. Der Broadway ist nun mal die repräsentativste Straße New Yorks, so wie der Kudamm in Berlin oder die Champs-Elysées in Paris. Das ist besser, als nur am Times Square herumzuhängen, da hat man bloß Touristen. Bist du in Harlem, hast du eine vollkommen unterschiedliche Wahrnehmung, und Soho ist anders als Tribeca. Wenn ich die Fifth Avenue herunterlaufe, habe ich einen komplett anderen Eindruck. Der Broadway ist als Querschnitt am interessantesten. Da hat man das gesamte Profil an Typen, an Gebäuden, an Kneipen, an Leuten mit Handys, Telefonhäuschen, Waschsalons, Delis, Zeitungskiosken und Nachtarbeitern. Einfach alles.

Was hat Sie am meisten fasziniert bei dem Lauf?

HH: Die ganze Atmosphäre, vor allem aber die Mischung: die Menschen, die Farben, das Durcheinander von Architektur und Lichtern und Leben und Energie und Rhythmus. Es war eben, wie einen Puls zu fühlen. Ich wollte nicht nur fotografisch ablichten, sondern die Stadt insgesamt spüren, richtig körperlich. Ich höre und rieche meine Bilder. New York nehme ich nie nur rein optisch wahr. Für mich ist es immer gleichzeitig ein akustisches Erlebnis, ein Geruchserlebnis, ein haptisches Erlebnis. Diese Stadt zu spüren, wie sie vibriert, wie die U-Bahn unter den Füßen grummelt, wie sich die Gerüche vermischen, das alles zusammen fasziniert mich. Zwölf Stunden Broadway ist das ideale Beispiel in so kompakter Zeit. Ich laufe und sprinte und ducke mich, um meine Fotos zu bekommen. Um mich herum ist das Sprachengewirr, das Theater und das Gehupe. Das geht mir gar nicht auf die Nerven, das habe ich schon immer geliebt. Das vermisse ich auch, sobald ich aus der Stadt heraus bin. Die Unterhaltungen mit den Menschen auf der Straße waren wie kurze Trips in verschiedene Lebensgeschichten. Am Schluß hatte ich sie wie Puzzlestücke zusammengewürfelt in meinem Kopf. Die Nacht am Broadway war wie ein Vitaminschub für mich. Eine New York-Injektion. Man sollte das als Therapie verordnen. Eigentlich sollte ich das jedes Jahr einmal tun: Andere laufen den Marathon, und ich laufe den Broadway herunter.

Welche Ausrüstung hatten Sie dabei?

HH: Ich bin mit zwei Digitalkameras von Leica, der Digilux 1, losgezogen. Ich habe neun Akkus verbraucht, weil die Kameras zwölf Stunden lang ununterbrochen an waren. Dazu 16 Speicherkarten mit insgesamt 2,3 Gigabytes. Während des Laufens habe ich immer mal Bilder gelöscht, um sicher zu gehen, daß die Karten ausreichen. Außerdem hatte ich einen Laptop dabei, damit ich zur Not Bilder darauf laden konnte. Wichtig für das Equipment sind übrigens auch gute Schuhe, das predige ich schon seit Jahren allen, die nach New York kommen: bequemes Schuhwerk.

Sind Sie die zwölf Stunden ohne Unterbrechung gelaufen?

HH: Wir haben zwischendrin nur ein paarmal Kaffee getrunken. Ich kann bei so einer Tour nichts essen, weil ich sonst umknicke. Ich wußte: Ich muß zwölf Stunden durchlaufen. Darauf hatte ich mich mental vorbereitet. Ich bin um 19.29 Uhr an der 125th Street losgelaufen und kam um 7.27 Uhr am nächsten Morgen im Battery Park an. Das allerletzte Foto war eigentlich kitschig, aber sehr symbolisch: ein Liebespaar, das sich in den Armen hält und auf die Freiheitsstatue schaut. Es war ein herrlicher Morgen, die Sonne ging auf, wir waren kreidebleich, aber happy. Von der mentalen Energie her hätten wir ohne Probleme zurücklaufen können. Rein körperlich waren wir aber am Ende.

Wie sind Sie, als Verfechter der traditionellen Fotografie, zur Digitalfotografie gekommen?

HH: Der Kolumnist der Tageszeitung *Newsday*, Jimmy Breslin, hatte die Geschichte geschrieben: "A Smile Gone, But Where?" Sein Sohn Kevin ist Regisseur und ein guter Freund von mir, ein echter New Yorker. Er faxte mir den Artikel seines Vaters und wollte die Geschichte nachdrehen. Vor sieben Jahren hatte ich mit ihm zusammen einen Aids-Aufklärungsfilm gemacht, der im Madison Square Garden gezeigt wurde. Seitdem hatte er mich öfter wegen eines weiteren gemeinsamen Filmprojekts gedrängt. Ich sagte immer, daß ich die Fotografie bevorzuge, aber wenn es etwas Interessantes gäbe, dann würde ich es mir überlegen. Die Story seines Vaters fand ich sehr stark, wegen der technischen Anforderungen hatte ich jedoch eine Höllenangst vor den Dreharbeiten bei Nacht. Trotzdem stimmte ich nach einigen erfolgreichen Probeaufnahmen mit einer digitalen Videokamera zu. Im November drehten wir dann eine Woche lang jede Nacht, von Sonnenuntergang bis Sonnenaufgang.

Danach hat es mich gepackt: Es war unglaublich, was Digitalkameras im Dunkeln leisten können, ich war schwer beeindruckt. Die Nachtschatten der Bäume oder Gullis, die man sonst nicht wahrnimmt, haben mich fasziniert. Dabei drehten wir in der 68th Street zwischen Amsterdam und Broadway, das ist ein ganz banaler Straßenblock mit der glatten, fensterlosen Seitenwand eines Kinos. Aber die Kamera übersetzt und verstärkt alle Details. Für mich war das wie eine Offenbarung: Ich war ja schon immer ein Nachtmensch, das konnte ich nur bis dahin fotografisch nie umsetzen. Aber jetzt. Am nächsten Tag bin ich sofort in meinen Fotoladen und kaufte mir eine Digitalkamera. Noch an Ort und Stelle ließ ich den Akku aufladen und legte sofort los.

Wie hat die digitale Technik Ihre Arbeit beeinflußt?

HH: Bei meinen Workshops am International Center of Photgraphy (ICP) in New York war ich immer der große Prediger für die analoge Fotografie. Aber ich wurde eines Besseren belehrt. Die Resultate waren einfach überzeugend, die haben mich regelrecht zu dem Broadway-Projekt inspiriert. Ab dem Zeitpunkt habe ich nachts nur noch digital fotografiert, egal wo ich war, ob in Paris, in New York oder Berlin.

Was ist an der Digitalfotografie so anders?

HH: Für mich ist die Digitalfotografie für so ein Projekt einfach ideal. Ich kann alles aus der Hand schießen – was meiner sonstigen Arbeitsweise sehr entspricht. Die Nachtaufnahmen hier wären mit einer traditionellen Kamera so gar nicht möglich, mit der muß man minutenlang belichten, mit Stativ und Drahtauslöser. Dann sind keine Menschen mehr drauf, weil alle ständig in Bewegung sind. Auf das Stativ habe ich ja auch schon bei dem Projekt *New York Vertical* verzichtet, dafür bin ich auf einen Film mit höherer Empfindlichkeit umgestiegen, weil ich gemerkt habe: Das Stativ behindert mich nur. Ich muß in Bewegung bleiben können, ich muß herumschleichen, herumtanzen können. Wenn ich das Stativ ständig aufstellen und einstellen muß, ist die Situation oft schon vorbei. Dann habe ich nach zwei Fotos keine Lust mehr.

Für dieses spezielle Projekt erwies sich die Digilux als das ideale Werkzeug, um den Anforderungen gerecht zu werden. Ich komponiere auf dem Bildschirm, ich schaue gar nicht mehr durch den Sucher. In der Nacht mischen sich die Farben. Man findet die verschiedensten Farbtemperaturen, die man mit dem bloßen Auge gar nicht erkennt: Kaltlicht wie von den Neonröhren der U-Bahn-Schächte, aber auch die ganze Palette an warmen Farbtönen, wie Gelb- und Rotlicht. In der Nacht kombiniert sich alles auf dem Bildschirm, die Kamera wird zum Pinsel. Für mich haben die Bilder wirklich etwas mit malen zu tun, regelrecht mit Licht einfangen.

Selected Exhibitions
Ausstellungen (Auswahl)

1980 *Cars and Stripes*, Fotografische Sammlung Bongartz, Krefeld
1984 *Bilder einer Ausstellung*, Künstlerhaus am Karlsplatz, Wien
1985 *Glaube, Liebe, Hoffnung*, Künstlerverband Bukarest, Bukarest
1985 Künstlerportraits, Kunsthaus Hamburg
1986 *Konfrontationen*, Ernst Museum, Budapest
1993 *Absolut Manhattan*, Nikon House, New York
1996 *New York Vertical*, Photokina, Köln
1998 *New York Vertical*, Nikon Image House, Zürich
1998/99 *New York Vertical*, Museum of the City of New York, New York
1999 *New York Vertical*, Internationale Fototage Herten
1999 *Neue Wege in der Industriefotografie*, Wilhelm-Hack-Museum, Ludwigshafen
2000 *Miniature*, Centre d'Art Microscopique, Paris
2000 *Verticals*, Vanderbilt Hall, Grand Central Terminal, New York
2001 *City*, Brooke Alexander Gallery, New York
2001 *Vertical View, 1991-2001*, Center for Maine Contemporary Arts, Rockport, Maine
2002 *Vertical View*, Galerie Kasten, Mannheim
2002 *Contrasts*, National Arts Club, New York
2002 *Horst Hamann: New York*, The Photographers Gallery, London
2002 *911*, Library of Congress, Washington
2002 *New York*, Michael Hoppen Gallery, London
2003 *Vertical View*, Galerie Kasten, Art Chicago
2003 *Die Neue Kunsthalle*, Kunsthalle Mannheim, Mannheim
2004 *New York Vertical*, Photobiennale Moskau
2004 *New York Vertical*, Gallery Ihn, Seoul
2005 *Paris Vertical*, Michael Hoppen Gallery, London

Selected Bibliography
Bibliographie (Auswahl)

1981 Marx, M.: „Eine individuelle Optik von Amerika", in: *Die Rheinpfalz*, Ludwigshafen/Rh. 12/81

1983 Prestele, Charly: „Ein Experiment der Gemeinschaft", in: *Mannheimer Morgen*, 5/83

1983 Wiedemann, Christoph: „Konfrontationen und Tonbilder", in: *Süddeutsche Zeitung*, München 5/83

1985 Bee, Andreas: „Die Unvordenklichkeit des Bildes bei Horst Hamann", in: Katalog *3.2.1. Raum auf Zeit*, Mannheim 1985

1988 Kiausch, Usch: „Zeitraum, Gleichzeitig - Gleichgültig?", in: *Communale*, Heidelberg 1988

1994 Hughes, Holly Stuart: „Horst Hamann loves New York", in: *Photo District News*, New York 4/94

1995 Klant, Michael: *Künstler bei der Arbeit von Fotografen gesehen*, Ostfildern-Ruit ´95

1996 Witte, Peter: „Ein Buch und sein Autor", in: *Photopresse*, Münden 42/96

1996 Klünder, Irene: „Wenn das Bauwerk das Format bestimmt", in: *Börsenblatt*, Frankfurt/Main 57/96

1996 Hess, Hans-Eberhard: „New York Vertical", in: *Photo Technik International*, München 9/96

1996 Langer, Freddy: „So hoch - Horst Hamann fotografiert New York", in: *FAZ - Frankfurter Allgemeine Zeitung* 227/96

1996 Langen, Andreas: „New York vertikal - die Wokenkratzer - City im Hochformat", in: *Stuttgarter Zeitung* 50/96

1996 „New York Vertical", in: *Bauwelt*, Berlin, Sonderheft 28/96

1997 Jst: „Ganz hoch hinaus", in: *Hannoverische Allgemeine Zeitung* 11/97

1997 Willemsen, Roger: „New York Vertical", in: *Vogue*, München 1/97

1997 Langen, Andreas: „New York Vertical", in: *Die Woche*, Hamburg 3/97

1997 Drommert, Jürgen: „New York Vertical", in: *Architektur & Wohnen*, Hamburg, New York spezial 2/97

1997 Weisman, Melissa A.: „Photographer Horst Hamann shoots for the top", in: *Hampton Country Magazine*, South Hampton 9/97

1997 Telford, Anne: „New York Vertical", in: *Communication Arts*, Palo Alto, CA 9/97

1997 „Look this way New York", in: *Daily News*, New York 12/97

1997 „New York Vertical", in: *Forbes Magazine*, New York 12/97

1997 Adams, Cindy: „New York Vertical Book Report", in: *New York Post* 12/97

1998 Klarwein-Milinaire, Serafine: „Horst Hamann", in: *Night Magazine*, New York 1/98

1998 MacNeille, Suzanne: „Head for Heights", in: *New York Times*, 3/98

1998 Pedersen, Anke: „Senkrecht-starter", in: *Wirtschaftswoche*, Düsseldorf 51/98

1999 Guttmann, Katja: „Horst Hamann / Portfolio", in: *Photographie* 7-8/99 und 9/99

1999 Heybrock, Christel: „Zwangloses Wechselspiel von Mensch und Mythos", in: *Mannheimer Morgen – Kultur* 215/99

1999 Berlinghof, Harald: „Neue Wege in der Industriefotografie", in: *Rhein-Neckar-Zeitung*, Heidelberg 9/99

1999 „Horst Hamann – Americana", in: *Photography Annual 40, Communication Arts*, Palo Alto, CA 8/99

1999 „Horst Hamann – New York Vertical", in: *Profi Foto*, Düsseldorf 9/99

1999 Zollner, Manfred: „Horst Hamann – Paris Vertical", Portfolio, in: *Foto Magazin*, München 11/99

1999 Hepae: „Die Krönung des bisherigen Fotofestivals", in: *Foto Contact*, 12/99

1999 Wagner, Thorsten: „New York Vertical von Horst Hamann in der Hertener Rundhalle setzt Maßstäbe", in: *Hertener Allgemeine* 7/99

1999 „New York Vertical", in: *Large Format*, Bochum 5/99

1999 G.U.: „Internationale Fototage Herten – Hamann's Inszenierung", in: *Photo Presse*, Hannoversch Münden 41/99

1999 Schelhorn, Tina: „The making of Big Apple", in: *Das Bild Forum*, Herten 7/99

2000 APO: „You can hold this sideways, too – NY Vertical", in: *Die Welt – Atlantic Daily*, Berlin/London/New York 4/00

2001 Saebisch, Babette: „Der Waghalsige unter den Fotografen", in: *Der Frankfurter* 3-4/01

2002 Miller, Alice: „One Night on Broadway", in: *Studio Photography and Design*, New York 11/02

2002 Jonckheer, Liz: „One Night on Broadway", in: *Photo District News*, New York 11/02

2003 Meers, Nick: „Panoramic Masters", in: *Stretch*, RotoVision, East Sussex 2003

2003 Graber, Bernd: „Trainspotting – Made in Germany", in: *Mannheimer Morgen* 8/03

2003 Dohnke, Kay: „Deutschland kreuz, Deutschland quer", in: *Mobil*, Hamburg 11/03

Selected TV Documentations & Radio Interviews
TV Dokumentationen & Radio Interviews (Auswahl)

1995 SDR 3, Süddeutscher Rundfunk TV
Klünder, Irene: „Portrait – Horst Hamann über New York", in: *Landesschau*, Stuttgart 1995

1996 WDR 3, Westdeutscher Rundfunk, Radio
Hoven, Herbert: „NY Vertical – ein Bildband von Horst Hamann", in: *Mosaik*, Köln 1996

1997 ARD, Süddeutscher Rundfunk TV
Krupok, Isolde: „Horst Hamann in New York", in: *Mensch, Leute!*, Stuttgart 1997

1997 ARTE – TV
Pütz, Günter: „Horst Hamann und seine vertikale Sichtweise", in: *Metropolis*, Strasbourg 1997

1998 ZDF Zweites Deutsches Fernsehen TV
Hess, Jutta: „New York im Hochformat – die Fotos von Horst Hamann", in: *Aspekte*, Mainz 1998

1998 SWF, Südwestfunk TV
Buettner, Tilmann: „Im Schatten der Wall Street", in: *USA*, Baden-Baden 1998

1998 WNBC – TV
Taylor, Felicia: „Horst Hamann at the Museum of the City of New York", in: *Sunday Today in New York*, New York 1998

1999 RNF – TV
Siegelmann, Bert: „Studiogast Horst Hamann", in: *Profil*, Mannheim 1999

1999 SWR, Südwestrundfunk TV
Kilwink, Isa: „Der Senkrecht-starter", in: *Nahaufnahme*, Mainz 1999

1999 BBC – TV
Potter, Elisabeth: „New York Vertical at the Museum of the City of New York", in: *BBC News*, New York – London 1999

1999 PBS – TV
Deroy, Jaimee: „Vertical Photographs at the Museum of the City of New York", in: *City Arts*, New York 1999

1999 RNF – TV
Boehm, Matthias: „Horst Hamann – Faces of a Company", in: *Landesschau*, Ludwigshafen 1999

1999 ARTE – TV
Burchardt, Melanie: „Big Apple bei den Fototagen in Herten", in: *Tracks*, Strasbourg 1999

1999 SWR 3 Südwestrundfunk Radio
Ries, Michael: „Studiogast Horst Hamann", in: *Leute*, Stuttgart 1999

1999 SWR – Südwestrundfunk TV
Hattensen, Maja: „Horst Hamann – Neue Wege in der Industrie-fotografie", in: *Kulturreport*, Mainz 1999

1999 SWR Südwestrundfunk TV
„Studiogast Horst Hamann“,
in: *Kultur Café*, Mainz 1999

1999 HR 3, Hessischer Rundfunk
& Fernsehen
Soliman, Tina: „Mr. Vertical“,
in: *Moderne Menschen*, Frankfurt
1999

2002 BBC Scotland
Live-Gäste (incl. Norman Mailer,
Horst Hamann) in: *Brian Morton
Show*, BBC Edinburgh/New York
1/02

2003 SWR Südwestrundfunk TV
„Panorma Deutsche Bahn,
Studiogast Horst Hamann“,
in: *Kultur Café*, Baden-Baden
10/03

Selected Films
Filme (Auswahl)

1995 *Urban Aid*
Madison Square Garden,
New York
Anti-AIDS-Kurzfilm: *They didn't know…*
(Kamera)

2001 *910-911 NYC*
Madison Square Garden,
New York
Kurzfilm, 8 Min.
(Buch, Regie, Kamera)

2001 *A Smile Gone, But Where?*
Nach einer Story von Jimmy
Breslin, mit Jimmy Breslin &
Karen Duffy
(Director of Photography)

Acknowledgments/Dank

marie, matéo, paolo

jimmy breslin
ronnie breslin

katja guttmann
adolfo doering
ax
nate cunningham
len stein
bernhard wipfler
wolfgang roth
robert and anne brochu
maria hamann
heinrich groeger
johannes hamann
matthias hamann
lutz bernstein
jochen rohner
werner bochmann
andrea and friedrich kasten
mike gregoire
roger conover
michael gray
ralf daab
leon kouyoumijian
andreas bee
jj straub
tilmann buettner
friedemann and ilona leinert
heike lang
jutta hess
udo van kampen
liz jonckheer

**thanks to all new yorkers
who crossed my path that night.**

**very special thanks to kevin breslin,
the true new yorker.**

for their generous support, thanks
to leica camera usa and germany
especially:
christian erhardt
ralf hagenauer
roger horn

and fred towns from panasonic

Den Essay von Jimmy Breslin übersetzten Katja Guttmann und
Marion Kagerer aus dem Amerikanischen.

Design: Robert Brochu
Lithos, Druck und Bindung: EBS, Verona

ISBN 3-8296-0127-1

Eine Schirmer/Mosel Produktion
www.schirmer-mosel.com

CATHERINE LANE

▸ 06:04:10

▸ 06:04:11

▸ 06:04:12

LEONARD STREET

▸ 06:01:15

▸ 06:01:16

▸ 06:01:17

▸ 06:01:18

▸ 06:01:19

FRANKLIN STREET

▸ 06:00:00

▸ 06:00:01

▸ 06:00:02

▸ 06:00:03

▸ 06:00:04

▸ 05:59:29

▸ 05:59:30

▸ 05:59:31

▸ 05:59:32

▸ 05:59:33

WALKER STREET

05:58:21

05:58:22

05:58:23

05:58:24

05:58:25

LISPENARD STREET

05:53:07

05:53:08

05:53:09

05:53:10

05:53:11

CANAL STREET

▸ 05:49:50

▸ 05:49:51

▸ 05:49:52

▸ 05:49:53

▸ 05:49:54

HOWARD STREET

▶ 05:43:23

▶ 05:43:24

▶ 05:43:25

▶ 05:43:26

▶ 05:43:27

GRAND STREET

▸ 05:40:36

▸ 05:40:37

▸ 05:40:38

▸ 05:40:39

BROOME STREET

▸ 05:30:16

▸ 05:30:17

▸ 05:30:18

▸ 05:30:19

▸ 05:30:20

SPRING STREET

▶ 05:29:31

▶ 05:29:32

▶ 05:29:33

▶ 05:29:34

▶ 05:29:35

PRINCE STREET

▸ 05:27:22

▸ 05:27:23

▸ 05:27:24

▸ 05:27:25

▸ 05:27:26

HOUSTON STREET

▸ 05:19:32

▸ 05:19:33

▸ 05:19:34

▸ 05:19:35

▸ 05:19:36

05:10:48

05:10:49

05:10:50

05:10:51

05:10:52

BOND STREET

▸ 05:04:45

▸ 05:04:46

▸ 05:04:47

▸ 05:04:48

▸ 05:04:49

▸ 05:04:50

▸ 05:04:51

▸ 05:01:47

▸ 05:01:48

▸ 05:01:49

▸ 05:01:50

ALDO

W 4th / E 4th
STREET

▶ 04:57:21

▶ 04:57:22

▶ 04:57:23

▶ 04:57:24

▶ 04:57:25

WASHINGTON PLACE

▸ 04:51:13

▸ 04:51:14

▸ 04:51:15

WAVERLY PLACE

▸ 04:45:25

▸ 04:45:26

▸ 04:45:27

▸ 04:45:28

▸ 04:45:29

ASTOR PLACE

▶ 04:39:57

▶ 04:39:58

▶ 04:39:59

▶ 04:40:00

▶ 04:40:01

8th STREET

▸ 04:35:26

▸ 04:35:27

▸ 04:35:28

▸ 04:35:29

▸ 04:35:30

▸ 04:34:38
▸ 04:34:39
▸ 04:34:40
▸ 04:34:41
▸ 04:34:42

10th STREET

- 04:27:26
- 04:27:27
- 04:27:28
- 04:27:29
- 04:27:30

11th STREET

▸ 04:20:35

▸ 04:20:36

▸ 04:20:37

▸ 04:20:38

▸ 04:20:39

12th STREET

- 04:16:01
- 04:16:02
- 04:16:03
- 04:16:04
- 04:16:05

13th STREET

▸ 04:06:14

▸ 04:06:15

▸ 04:06:16

▸ 04:06:17

▸ 04:06:18

14th STREET / UNION SQUARE

▸ 03:53:29

▸ 03:53:30

▸ 03:53:31

▸ 03:53:32

▸ 03:53:33

E 15th STREET / UNION SQUARE

▸ 03:48:55

▸ 03:48:56

▸ 03:48:57

▸ 03:48:58

▸ 03:48:59

16th STREET / UNION SQUARE

▸ 03:45:35

▸ 03:45:36

▸ 03:45:37

▸ 03:45:38

▸ 03:45:39

17th STREET / UNION SQUARE

▸ 03:42:51

▸ 03:42:52

▸ 03:42:53

▸ 03:42:54

▸ 03:42:55

18th STREET

▸ 03:39:40

▸ 03:39:41

▸ 03:39:42

BROADWAY
FUTON

19th STREET

▸ 03:35:46

▸ 03:35:47

▸ 03:35:48

▸ 03:35:49

▸ 03:35:50

20th STREET

▸ 03:33:39

▸ 03:33:40

▸ 03:33:41

▸ 03:33:42

▸ 03:33:43

21st STREET

▸ 03:31:59

▸ 03:32:00

▸ 03:32:01

22nd STREET

- 03:30:02
- 03:30:03
- 03:30:04
- 03:30:05
- 03:30:06

23rd STREET

▸ 03:27:33

▸ 03:27:34

▸ 03:27:35

No entry
Enter at 23 St & 5 A

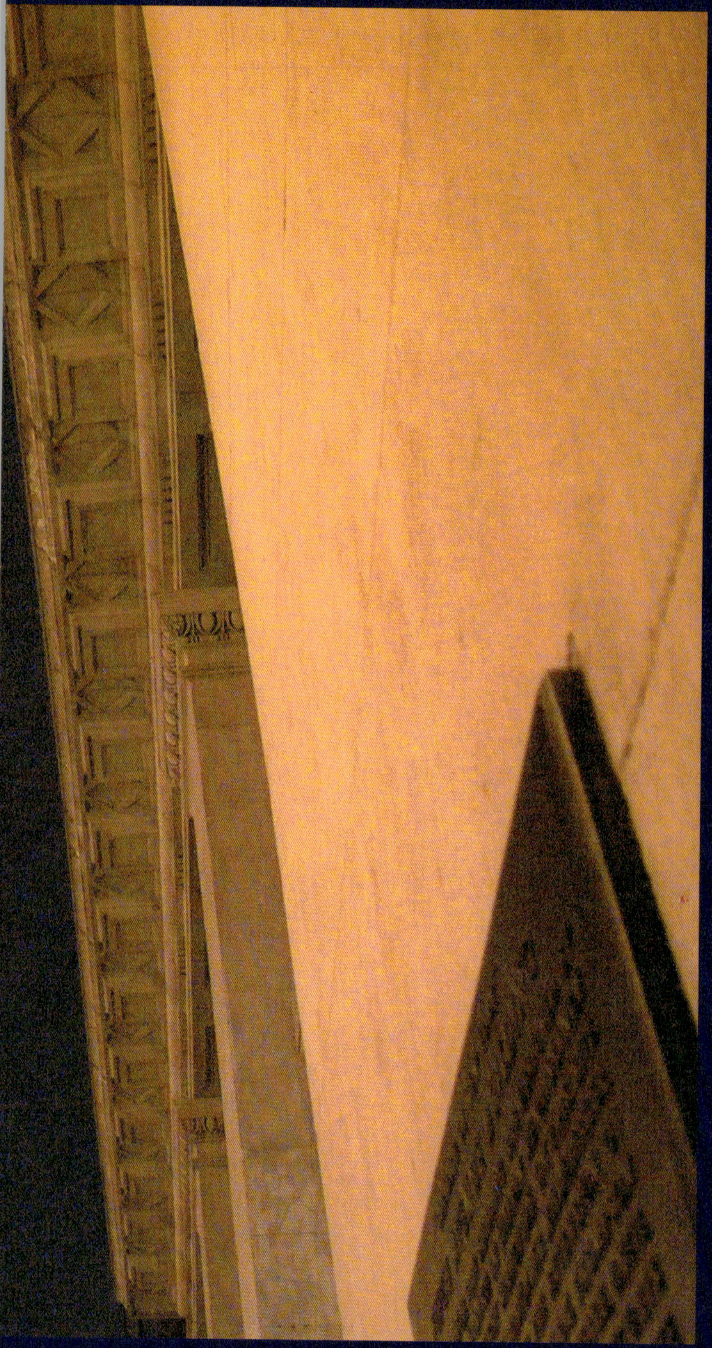

24th STREET

▶ 03:23:09

▶ 03:23:10

▶ 03:23:11

▶ 03:23:12

▶ 03:23:13

25th STREET

▸ 03:19:48

▸ 03:19:49

▸ 03:19:50

▸ 03:19:51

▸ 03:19:52

26th STREET

▸ 03:17:43

▸ 03:17:44

▸ 03:17:45

▸ 03:17:46

▸ 03:17:47

27th STREET

▸ 03:15:57

▸ 03:15:58

▸ 03:15:59

▸ 03:16:00

▸ 03:16:01

28th STREET

▶ 03:13:19

▶ 03:13:20

▶ 03:13:21

▶ 03:13:22

▶ 03:13:23

29th STREET

▸ 03:11:54

▸ 03:11:55

▸ 03:11:56

▸ 03:11:57

▸ 03:11:58

30th STREET

▸ 03:11:00

▸ 03:11:01

▸ 03:11:02

▸ 03:11:03

▸ 03:11:04

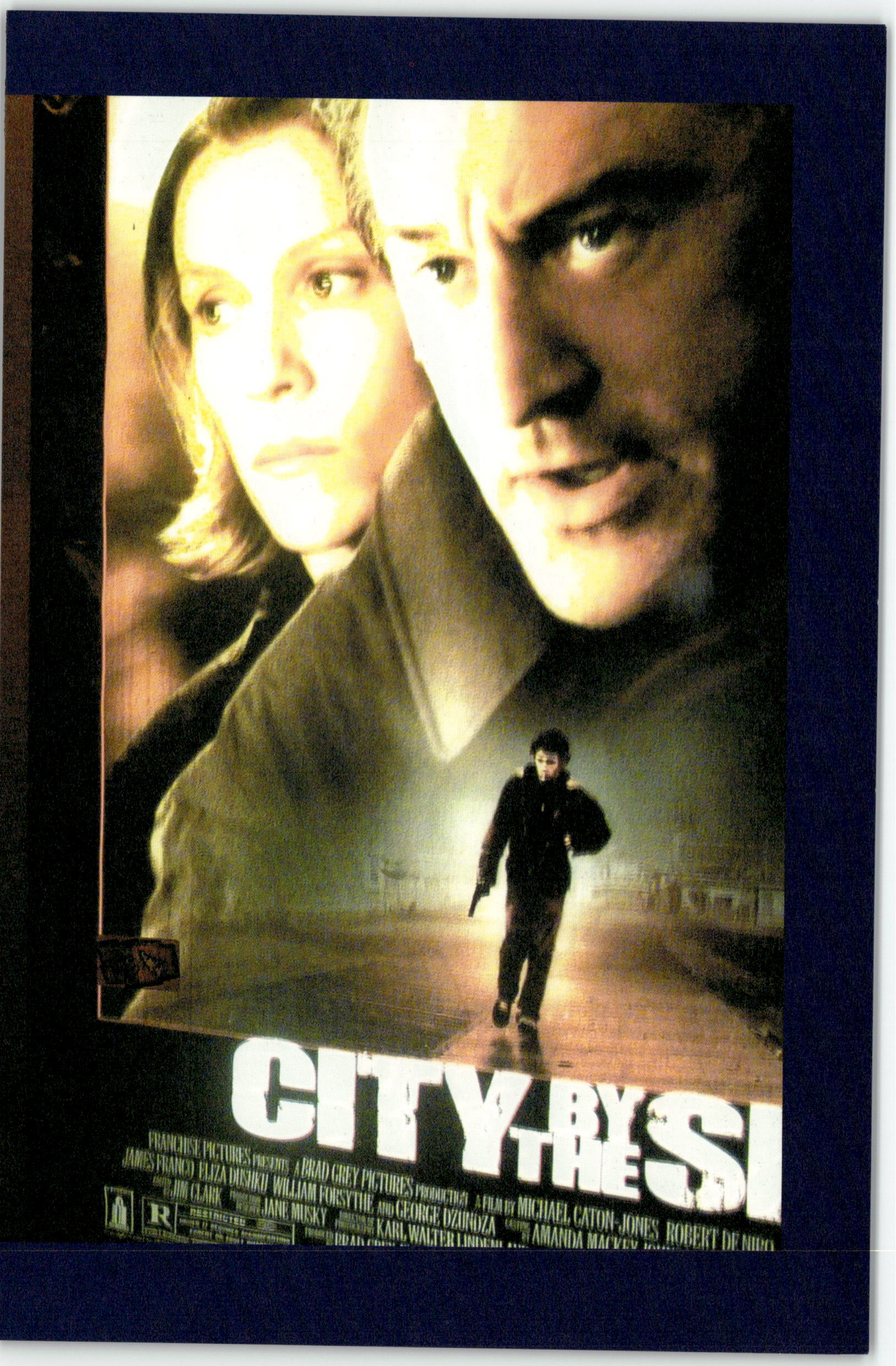
CITY BY THE S
FRANCHISE PICTURES PRESENTS A BRAD GREY PICTURES PRODUCTION
JAMES FRANCO ELIZA DUSHKU WILLIAM FORSYTHE AND GEORGE DZUNDZA
JIM CLARK
JANE MUSKY
KARL WALTER LINDENLAUB
A FILM BY MICHAEL CATON-JONES ROBERT DE NIRO
AMANDA MACKEY
R
RESTRICTED

31st STREET

▸ 03:09:53
▸ 03:09:54
▸ 03:09:55
▸ 03:09:56
▸ 03:09:57

32nd STREET /
KOREA WAY

▸ 03:07:14

▸ 03:07:15

▸ 03:07:16

33rd STREET

▸ 02:55:06

▸ 02:55:07

▸ 02:55:08

▸ 02:55:09

▸ 02:55:10

34th STREET / HERALD SQUARE

▸ 02:48:38

▸ 02:48:39

▸ 02:48:40

▸ 02:48:41

▸ 02:48:42

35th STREET

▸ 02:12:30

▸ 02:12:31

▸ 02:12:32

▸ 02:12:33

▸ 02:12:34

36th STREET

▸ 02:05:47

▸ 02:05:48

▸ 02:05:49

▸ 02:05:50

▸ 02:05:51

37th STREET

▸ 01:57:53
▸ 01:57:54
▸ 01:57:55
▸ 01:57:56
▸ 01:57:57

30%

38th STREET

▸ 01:50:38

▸ 01:50:39

▸ 01:50:40

▸ 01:50:41

▸ 01:50:42

39th STREET

▸ 01:49:13

▸ 01:49:14

▸ 01:49:15

▸ 01:49:16

▸ 01:49:17

40th STREET

▸ 01:42:40

▸ 01:42:41

▸ 01:42:42

▸ 01:42:43

▸ 01:42:44

▸ 01:42:45

41st STREET

▸ 01:39:35

▸ 01:39:36

▸ 01:39:37

▸ 01:39:38

▸ 01:39:39

42nd STREET

▸ 01:35:21

▸ 01:35:22

▸ 01:35:23

▸ 01:35:24

▸ 01:35:25

43rd /
ADOLPH S.
OCHS STREET

▸ 01:27:07
▸ 01:27:08
▸ 01:27:09
▸ 01:27:10
▸ 01:27:11

soni
NEW YOR

44th STREET /
GOOD MORNING
AMERICA WAY

▸ 01:24:08
▸ 01:24:09
▸ 01:24:10
▸ 01:24:11
▸ 01:24:12

SEPT. 11, EVEN THOUG
ROD WASHBURN IS UND
USA TODAY

45th STREET / GEORGE ABBOTT WAY

▶ 01:17:54

▶ 01:17:55

▶ 01:17:56

▶ 01:17:57

▶ 01:17:58

46th /
LITTLE BRAZIL
STREET

▸ 01:09:27

▸ 01:09:28

▸ 01:09:29

▸ 22:09:30

▸ 22:09:31

47th STREET / DUFFY SQUARE

▸ 01:03:16

▸ 01:03:17

▸ 01:03:18

▸ 01:03:19

▸ 01:03:20

48th STREET

▸ 12:48:17

▸ 12:48:18

▸ 12:48:19

▸ 12:48:20

▸ 12:48:21

49th STREET

- 12:46:53
- 12:46:54
- **12:46:55**
- 12:46:56
- 12:46:57

50th STREET

▸ 12:41:03

▸ 12:41:04

▸ 12:41:05

▸ 12:41:06

▸ 12:41:07

51st STREET

- ▸ 12:37:47
- ▸ 12:37:48
- ▸ 12:37:49
- ▸ 12:37:50
- ▸ 12:37:51

52nd STREET

▸ 12:29:49

▸ 12:29:50

▸ 12:29:51

▸ 12:29:52

▸ 12:29:53

▸ 12:26:05

▸ 12:26:06

▸ 12:26:07

▸ 12:26:08

54th STREET

- 12:24:27
- 12:24:28
- 12:24:29
- 12:24:30
- 12:24:31

55th STREET

▸ 12:21:39

▸ 12:21:40

▸ 12:21:41

▸ 12:21:42

▸ 12:21:43

56th STREET

▸ 12:20:02

▸ 12:20:03

▸ 12:20:04

▸ 12:20:05

▸ 12:20:06

57th STREET

▸ 12:19:04

▸ 12:19:05

▸ 12:19:06

▸ 12:19:07

▸ 12:19:08

58th STREET

▸ 12:17:48

▸ 12:17:49

▸ 12:17:50

▸ 12:17:51

▸ 12:17:52

59th STREET

▸ 12:14:02
▸ 12:14:03
▸ 12:14:04
▸ 12:14:05
▸ 12:14:06

60th STREET

▸ 12:10:05

▸ 12:10:06

▸ 12:10:07

▸ 12:10:08

▸ 12:10:09

61st STREET

▸ 12:08:10
▸ 12:08:11
▸ 12:08:12
▸ 12:08:13
▸ 12:08:14

62nd STREET

▸ 12:06:05
▸ 12:06:06
▸ 12:06:07

GREEN
SIGNAL
WAY

63rd STREET

▸ 12:01:45

▸ 12:01:46

▸ 12:01:47

▸ 12:01:48

▸ 12:01:49

64th STREET

▸ 12:00:17

▸ 12:00:18

▸ 12:00:19

▸ 12:00:20

▸ 12:00:21

65th STREET / LEONARD BERNSTEIN PLACE

▸ 11:58:06

▸ 11:58:07

▸ 11:58:08

▸ 11:58:09

▸ 11:58:10

66th STREET

▸ 11:56:30

▸ 11:56:31

▸ 11:56:32

67th STREET

▸ 11:52:27

▸ 11:52:28

▸ 11:52:29

▸ 11:52:30

▸ 11:52:31

RECO
FROM TH

NCOLN

68th STREET

▸ 11:49:49

▸ 11:49:50

▸ 11:49:51

69th STREET

▸ 11:45:29

▸ 11:45:30

▸ 11:45:31

▸ 11:45:32

▸ 11:45:33

70th STREET

▸ 11:40:38

▸ 11:40:39

▸ 11:40:40

▸ 11:40:41

▸ 11:40:42

▸ 11:37:38

▸ 11:37:39

▸ 11:37:40

▸ 11:37:41

72nd STREET

▸ 11:28:04

▸ 11:28:05

▸ 11:28:06

▸ 11:28:07

▸ 11:28:08

73rd STREET

▸ 11:15:20
▸ 11:15:21
▸ **11:15:22**
▸ 11:15:23
▸ 11:15:24

12
1
2
3

74th STREET

▸ 11:13:19

▸ 11:13:20

▸ 11:13:21

▸ 11:13:22

▸ 11:13:23

ALL
EXITS
FINAL

75th STREET

▸ 11:11:12

▸ 11:11:13

▸ 11:11:14

▸ 11:11:15

▸ 11:11:16

76th STREET

▶ [illegible]

▶ 11:07:46

▶ 11:07:47

▶ 11:07:48

▶ 11:07:49

▶ 11:07:50

▶ [illegible]

77th STREET

▸ 11:05:58

▸ 11:05:59

▸ 11:06:00

▸ 11:06:01

▸ 11:06:02

78th STREET

▸ 10:58:28

▸ 10:58:29

▸ 10:58:30

79th STREET

▸ 10:55:04
▸ 10:55:05
▸ 10:55:06
▸ 10:55:07
▸ 10:55:08

80th STREET

▸ 10:52:28

▸ 10:52:29

▸ 10:52:30

▸ 10:52:31

▸ 10:52:32

81st STREET

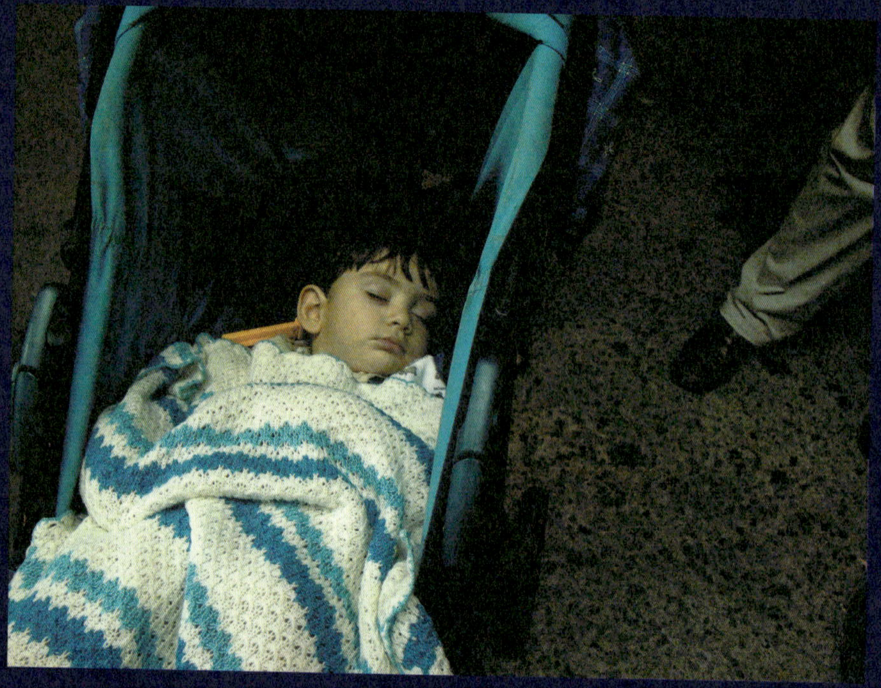

▸ 10:50:32

▸ 10:50:33

▸ 10:50:34

▸ 10:50:35

▸ 10:50:36

82nd STREET

▸ 10:48:16

▸ 10:48:17

▸ 10:48:18

▸ 10:48:19

▸ 10:48:20

▸ 10:45:37
▸ 10:45:38
▸ 10:45:39
▸ 10:45:40
▸ 10:45:41

84th STREET

▸ 10:44:55

▸ 10:44:56

▸ 10:44:57

▸ 10:44:58

▸ 10:44:59

85th STREET

▸ 10:42:57

▸ 10:42:58

▸ 10:42:59

▸ 10:43:00

▸ 10:43:01

ALFRED

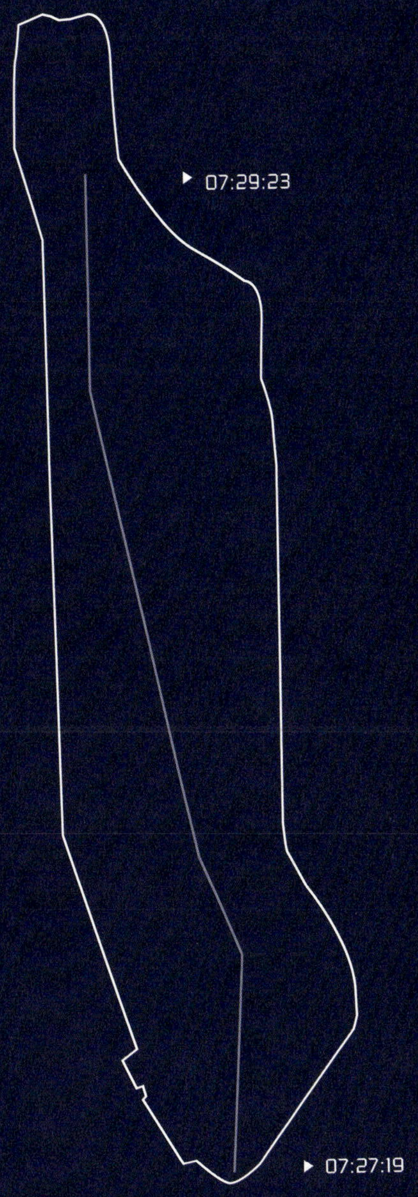
▸ 07:29:23
▸ 07:27:19

The Big Street
by Jimmy Breslin

Celandia stood at her checkout station at the Food Emporium store on the corner of Broadway and West 68th Street and stared out at the start of dawn on Broadway. It was not crowded at this hour of a Sunday morning in the late spring. Nor was it empty. Any emptiness was immediately interspersed by traffic moving downtown in a creek of red taillights.

She was in her green supermarket jacket. She looked over the traffic and at the blue sign blazing in the last of the night. It was over the Commerce bank, and the neon shouted that the bank is open seven days a week.

"I wish I could go there to work," she was saying. "I was supposed to take the test on Friday. But I didn't go."

"Why not?"

"I had to go to my second job. Columbia Presbyterian hospital. I do food service. I'm on probation. I finish my probation they give me full time. Right now, I still don't have for my daughter day care."

Her hospital job was a full hundred blocks uptown on Broadway. It was the second location on the most famous street in the world for her struggle in life. The first was here in this supermarket where she could look out and see the Lincoln Center opera house. There are nights when she starts her job that the lights of the opera house mesmerize her and last through the night in the memory of her eyes. Directly across the sidestreet, 68th, is the red glow of the marquee of the movie house that makes the most money of any house in the world. It has 25 theatres. Every week, a red carpet is out and searchlights sweep the sky for stars coming out of limousines for their picture's opening.

This is the street of trying. The old saying was that there was a broken heart for every light on Broadway. That is not true by half. Straight down the street from the supermarket, down in the 40's, where the street opens to a fully lighted sky, people sit in bare rooms on the sidestreets reading for parts in plays and movies while casting people sit at the tables and listen to the reading and then say, "Thank you" and the actor walks out and knows he'll never hear from them again, but simultaneously he has the picture in his mind of his roommate saying, "You got a call back."

Here, too, Garson Kanin and Jules Styne sit at a table in a darkened theatre and watch Barbra Streisand read a little, sing a little before being cut off by the two who openly fear that she will walk out of theatre on them. Their show is "Funny Girl." Their star, their international star, their star forever, is right here in front of them. Ms. Streisand.

The sidewalks carry the memories of old crapshooters and the throngs for today's "Lion King." Straight down, Broadway and Seventh Avenue split and you come onto these large buildings that seem gloomy but actually mask the circus of the world's clothing, the New York garment district. Trucks jam the sidestreets. Men weave through traffic, pushing racks of clothes. And all through the buildings, the line moves at Bergdorf's, it lags at Bloomingdale's, my buttons are great, my belts are wonderful, my shirt designer is a nice guy but he has too many boyfriends, I have to go to my factor's anniversary party out in Great Neck.

The sidewalks are filled and the subways below run swift and crowded and always on time. Broadway now runs down through stretches of Arab stores, and now it comes to Bleecker and Broadway, where a man gives haircuts on a chair he puts on the sidewalk, where the large crowds of Chinese buy food at stores for one meal at a time, where crowds march between office buildings, and now you come to City Hall, which is the only place in the city that seems nervous about the times in which we live. There are preposterous gates and barricades that come out of the ground to stop cars. People must walk through metal detectors. The people going into City Hall and the large crowds passing by are not nervous. It is the police and politicians, who live in paranoia and want to control all, who act as if they know of an attack coming tomorrow.

The street runs past a famous church, St. Paul's Chapel, and suddenly here is the vacant land of what was the World Trade Center. People stare through fencing at the emptiness on the other side. The news reports are always filled with tales of people who need psychological help because of the attacks. Most of them would give up their appointments in exchange for a job. There is no help required by those still turning over millions on the streets off the World Trade Center site.

Still, it is too real for Lauri Koelle, who worked at an employment agency on Broadway, directly across the street from the World Trade Center. On September 11, 2001, she was walking her son, Frankie, home from school on Bleecker Street because the towers were on fire. Suddenly, the first tower exploded. She ran with her son to their home on First Avenue. All these months later, her son stares out his bedroom window. Once, he could see the World Trade Center towers. Now he sees a blank sky. He draws rectangles and has them blowing up.

"Is this how it looked, daddy?" he asks. "Is this how it looked?"

Aside from Frankie Koelle's pictures, the bombings changed only the skyline but not the people I know. For them the brass bands playing for success or the ceaseless struggles go on.

And Celandia stands in the supermarket on 68th and Broadway and says, "I was so sad Friday. You wouldn't believe how sad I was. It's still so sad right now."

"Why?"

"I went to the day care to put my daughter in. They said no. I make too much for my two jobs." She pronounced it "yobs."

"I started to cry. I wanted my daughter in day care so bad. I leave her with my mother when I work. I wanted her to get out, to learn more. My mother doesn't speak English." They are from the "DR", or Dominican Republic.

"What do they call making too much?" she was asked. "Something two thousand. The month. They counted the whole. Two jobs. They don't asking about the taxes and rent. Pampers and milk. I have to support me and my daughter. We live with my mother. How can I have too much money?"

She is 31 and short and has her hair tied back. She has a lovely round face and large brown eyes.

She nodded at the bank across Broadway.

"I want to take the test for the bank," she said. "It is better job than here. You get full-time. All the benefits."

"You don't get that here?"

"Not if you're part time. Thirteen years I'm part-time here. I ask them for full-time job for the benefits and they say, we have no job now. Thirteen years they say that."

"What do they pay?"

"Ten dollar an hour. I say I want a raise. To thirteen. They say they can't do that now. I have to wait. I have to wait ten more years for a raise. Checkout girls don't get anything. This is very hard, living on Broadway. Sometimes it is so beautiful. You think you can become rich by working hard. Then it is cold and you don't have money for your daughter's day care."

The Big Street
von Jimmy Breslin

Celandia stand an ihrer Kasse des Food Emporium, Ecke Broadway und West 68th Street, und starrte in die beginnende Morgendämmerung am Broadway. Zu dieser Tageszeit, an einem Sonntag im Spätfrühling, war dort nicht viel los. Der Broadway war aber auch nicht leer. Jedes freie Fleckchen wurde sofort vom Verkehr in Beschlag genommen, der sich in einem Strom roter Rücklichter Richtung Downtown bewegte.

Sie hatte ihren grünen Supermarkt-Kittel an. Sie blickte über den Verkehr auf das blaue Neonschild, das im letzten Dunkel der Nacht grell leuchtete. Es hing über der Commerce-Bank und verkündete schrill, daß die Bank sieben Tage die Woche offen sei.

„Dort würde ich gerne arbeiten", sagte sie. „Am Freitag hätte ich eigentlich den Einstellungstest machen sollen. Aber dann bin ich nicht hingegangen."

„Warum nicht?"

„Weil ich zu meinem zweiten Job mußte. Im Columbia Presbyterian Hospital. Ich teile Essen aus. Ich bin dort auf Probe. Nach der Probezeit kann ich Vollzeit arbeiten. Ich habe immer noch keine Tagesstätte für meine Tochter."

Ihr Krankenhaus-Job war auch am Broadway, volle hundert Blocks nördlich. Der zweite Ort an der berühmtesten Straße der Welt, an dem sie sich abrackerte. Der erste war hier im Supermarkt, wo sie zur Oper im Lincoln Center hinüberschauen konnte. In manchen Nächten, wenn sie anfängt zu arbeiten, ist sie wie hypnotisiert von den Lichtern des Opernhauses, die für den Rest der Nacht vor ihren Augen nachglimmen. Direkt gegenüber in der Seitenstraße, der 68th Street, leuchtet rot das Vordach des Kinos, das von allen Kinos der Welt den größten Profit macht. Es hat fünfundzwanzig Säle. Jede Woche wird der rote Teppich ausgerollt und Scheinwerfer schwenken über den Himmel auf Stars, die zur Premiere ihres Films aus den Limousinen steigen.

Am Broadway versuchen die Menschen ihr Glück. Ein altes Sprichwort sagt, auf jedes Licht am Broadway kommt ein gebrochenes Herz. Und das ist erst die halbe Wahrheit. Südlich vom Supermarkt, unten in den 40ern, wo sich der Broadway zu einem hell erleuchteten Himmel hin öffnet, sitzen Leute in kahlen Räumen in den Seitenstraßen und sprechen für Rollen in Theaterstücken und Filmen vor. Die Casting-Agenten sitzen an Tischen, hören sich das Vorsprechen an und sagen „danke", und der Schauspieler geht und weiß, daß er nie wieder etwas von ihnen hören wird, aber gleichzeitig hat er die Szene im Kopf, wie sein Mitbewohner sagt: „Sie haben angerufen".

Hier sitzen auch Garson Kanin und Jules Styne an einem Tisch in einem abgedunkelten Theater und schauen Barbra Streisand zu, wie sie ein bißchen vorliest, ein bißchen vorsingt, bevor sie von den beiden unterbrochen wird. Und man sieht ihnen die Angst an, sie könnte einfach aufstehen und gehen. Ihre Show heißt *Funny Girl*. Ihr Star, ihr internationaler Star, ihr Star für alle Ewigkeit, steht vor ihnen, Ms. Streisand.

Die Gehsteige tragen Erinnerungen an die Würfelspieler von damals und das Gedränge um den „Lion King" von heute. Weiter südlich gabeln sich Broadway und Seventh Avenue, und man trifft auf die großen Gebäude, die düster wirken, aber eigentlich nur den Modezirkus der Welt tarnen: den New York Garment Dirstrict. Laster blockieren die Seitenstraßen. Männer schlängeln sich durch den Verkehr, schieben Kleiderständer vor sich her. Und von allen Gebäuden bewegt sich die Schlange Richtung Bergdorf's, bremst bei Bloomingdale's, meine Knöpfe sind spitze, meine Gürtel sind ein Traum, mein Hemden-Designer ist ein echt netter Kerl, aber er hat zu viele Liebhaber, ich muß zur Jubiläumsfeier meines Vertreters nach Great Neck.

Die Gehsteige sind voll, und die U-Bahnen fahren eilig darunter weg, überfüllt und immer pünktlich. Der Broadway führt jetzt an einer ganzen Zeile arabischer Läden vorbei und kreuzt Bleeker Street, wo ein Mann einen Stuhl auf den Gehsteig stellt und den Leuten die Haare schneidet, wo es vor Chinesen wimmelt, die für jede Mahlzeit einzeln einkaufen, wo Menschenmengen zwischen Bürogebäuden durchmarschieren. Und jetzt kommt man zur City Hall. Es scheint der einzige Ort in der Stadt zu sein, wo man nervös ist angesichts der Zeiten, in denen wir leben. Dort sprießen groteske Sperren und Barrikaden aus dem Boden, um Autos zu stoppen. Besucher müssen durch Metalldetektoren laufen. Die Bürger, die ins Rathaus wollen, und die Menschenmengen, die daran vorbeilaufen, sind nicht nervös. Nur die Polizisten und Politiker sind paranoid und wollen alles kontrollieren, tun so, als wüßten sie, daß es morgen einen Anschlag gibt.

Der Broadway führt an der berühmten St. Paul's Chapel vorbei, und plötzlich steht man vor dem Loch, wo früher das World Trade Center war. Leute starren durch Absperrungen in die Ödnis auf der anderen Seite. Die Nachrichten sind voll von Berichten über Menschen, die wegen der Anschläge psychologische Hilfe brauchen. Die meisten würden ihren Termin beim Therapeuten liebend gerne gegen einen Job eintauschen. Diejenigen, die in den Straßen rund ums World Trade Center weiter Millionen scheffeln, brauchen keine Therapie.

Für Lauri Koelle, die in einer Zeitarbeitsfirma am Broadway gearbeitet hat, direkt gegenüber vom World Trade Center, ist das alles noch viel zu real. Am 11. September brachte sie gerade ihren Sohn Frankie von der Schule in der Bleeker Street nach Hause, weil die Türme brannten. Plötzlich explodierte der erste Turm. Sie rannte mit ihrem Sohn nach Hause, in die First Avenue. Jetzt, viele Monate später, sitzt ihr Sohn im Kinderzimmer und schaut aus dem Fenster. Früher konnte er von dort die Türme des World Trade Center sehen. Jetzt sieht er den leeren Himmel. Er malt Rechtecke und läßt sie explodieren. „War es so, Papa?", fragt er. „Hat das so ausgesehen?"

Abgesehen von Frankie Koelles Bildern haben die Anschläge nur die Skyline verändert, aber nicht die Menschen, die ich kenne. Für sie spielt die Band weiter einen Tusch auf ihre Erfolge, geht das endlose Rackern weiter.

Und Celandia steht im Supermarkt Ecke 68th und Broadway und sagt: „Letzten Freitag war ich echt deprimiert. Sie glauben gar nicht, wie deprimiert ich war. Ich bin immer noch deprimiert."

„Warum?"

„Ich wollte meine Tochter in der Tagesstätte anmelden. Sie haben sie nicht genommen. Ich verdiene zuviel mit meinen zwei Jobs." Sie sprach das Wort „Yobs" aus.

„Ich fing an zu heulen. Ich wollte doch unbedingt, daß meine Tochter in eine Tagesstätte kommt. Ich lasse sie bei meiner Mutter, wenn ich arbeite. Ich wollte, daß sie rauskommt, daß sie mehr lernt. Meine Mutter spricht kein Englisch." Sie sind von der „DR", der Dominikanischen Republik.

„Was verstehen die unter ‚zuviel'?", wurde sie gefragt. „So um die zweitausend. Im Monat. Sie haben alles zusammengezählt. Zwei Jobs. Sie haben nicht nach Steuern und Miete gefragt. Windeln und Milch. Ich muß mich und meine Tochter durchbringen. Wir leben bei meiner Mutter. Wie sollte ich zuviel verdienen?"

Sie ist einunddreißig und klein und hat sich die Haare zurückgebunden. Sie hat ein hübsches, rundes Gesicht und große braune Augen.

Sie deutete mit dem Kinn auf die gegenüberliegende Straßenseite.

„Ich möchte den Einstellungstest für die Bank machen", sagte sie. „Der Job ist besser als hier. Man bekommt einen Vollzeit-Job und alle Sozialleistungen."

„Hier nicht?"

„Nicht, wenn man Teilzeit arbeitet. Ich bin hier schon seit dreizehn Jahren auf Teilzeit. Ich bitte um einen Vollzeit-Job, wegen der Sozialleistungen, und sie sagen: Wir haben gerade keine Stelle frei. Seit dreizehn Jahren sagen sie das."

„Was zahlen sie denn?"

„Zehn Dollar die Stunde. Ich verlange eine Lohnerhöhung. Auf dreizehn. Sie sagen, das geht momentan nicht. Ich soll warten. Ich muß wohl nochmal zehn Jahre auf eine Lohnerhöhung warten. Kassiererinnen bekommen nichts. Der Broadway ist ein rauhes Pflaster. Manchmal ist es hier wunderschön. Du denkst, du kannst reich werden, wenn du nur hart arbeitest. Aber dann ist es wieder kalt, und du hast nicht mal Geld für die Tagesstätte deiner Tochter."

DONT
WALK
WALK

125th STREET

▸ 07:29:21

▸ 07:29:22

▸ 07:29:23

▸ 07:29:24

▸ 07:29:25

TIEMANN PLACE

▶ 07:36:57

▶ 07:36:58

▶ 07:36:59

▶ 07:37:00

▶ 07:37:01

LA SALLE STREET

▸ 07:43:03

▸ 07:43:04

▸ 07:43:05

▸ 07:43:06

▸ 07:43:07

123rd STREET

▸ 07:50:49

▸ 07:50:50

▸ 07:50:51

▸ 07:50:52

▸ 07:50:53

SEMINARY ROW

▸ 07:54:11

▸ 07:54:12

▸ 07:54:13

▸ 07:54:14

▸ 07:54:15

121st STREET

▸ 07:56:14

▸ 07:56:15

▸ 07:56:16

▸ 07:56:17

▸ 07:56:18

BROA

120th STREET

▶ 07:58:29

▶ 07:58:30

▶ 07:58:31

119th STREET

▸ 08:01:17

▸ 08:01:18

▸ 08:01:19

▸ 08:01:20

▸ 08:01:21

118th STREET

- 08:03:28
- 08:03:29
- 08:03:30
- 08:03:31
- 08:03:32

▸ 08:10:33

▸ 08:10:34

▸ 08:10:35

▸ 08:10:36

▸ 08:10:37

116th STREET

▸ 08:26:00
▸ 08:26:01
▸ 08:26:02
▸ 08:26:03
▸ 08:26:04

115th STREET

▶ 08:39:43

▶ 08:39:44

▶ 08:39:45

114th STREET

- 08:49:32
- 08:49:33
- 08:49:34
- 08:49:35
- 08:49:36

▸ 08:53:06

▸ 08:53:07

▸ 08:53:08

▸ 08:53:09

▸ 08:53:10

▸ 08:56:43

▸ 08:56:44

▸ 08:56:45

▸ 08:56:46

▸ 08:56:47

▸ 08:59:29

▸ 08:59:30

▸ 08:59:31

▸ 08:59:32

▸ 08:59:33

110th STREET / CATHEDRAL PARKWAY

- 09:06:06
- 09:06:07
- 09:06:08
- 09:06:09
- 09:06:10

▸ 09:10:00
▸ 09:10:01
▸ 09:10:02
▸ 09:10:03
▸ 09:10:04

108th STREET

▸ 09:16:43
▸ 09:16:44
▸ 09:16:45
▸ 09:16:46
▸ 09:16:47

107th STREET

▸ 09:26:44

▸ 09:26:45

▸ 09:26:46

▸ 09:26:47

▸ 09:26:48

106th STREET / DUKE ELLINGTON BOULEVARD

▸ 09:34:37

▸ 09:34:38

▸ 09:34:39

▸ 09:34:40

▸ 09:34:41

105th STREET

▸ 09:41:06

▸ 09:41:07

▸ 09:41:08

▸ 09:41:09

▸ 09:41:10

104th STREET

▸ 09:45:09

▸ 09:45:10

▸ 09:45:11

▸ 09:45:12

▸ 09:45:13

103rd STREET

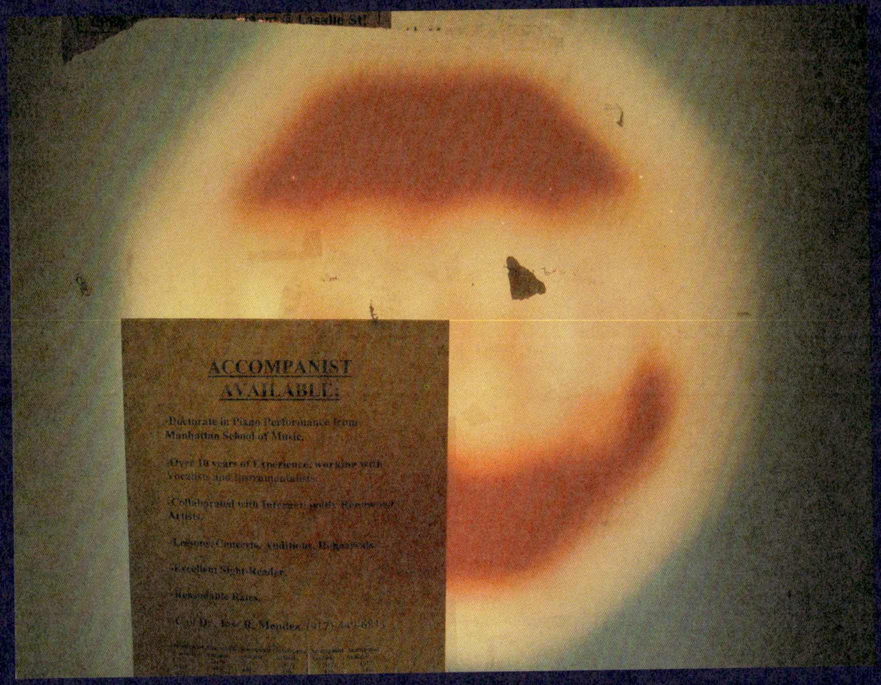

▸ 09:48:47

▸ 09:48:48

▸ 09:48:49

▸ 09:48:50

▸ 09:48:51

▸ 09:51:10

▸ 09:51:11

▸ 09:51:12

▸ 09:51:13

▸ 09:51:14

▸ 09:54:25

▸ 09:54:26

▸ 09:54:27

▸ 09:54:28

▸ 09:54:29

100th STREET

▸ 09:58:49

▸ 09:58:50

▸ 09:58:51

▸ 09:58:52

▸ 09:58:53

▸ 09:59:48

▸ 09:59:49

▸ 09:59:50

▸ 09:59:51

▸ 09:59:52

▸ 10:02:17

▸ 10:02:18

▸ 10:02:19

▸ 10:02:20

▸ 10:02:21

97th STREET

▸ 10:06:02
▸ 10:06:03
▸ 10:06:04
▸ 10:06:05
▸ 10:06:06

96th STREET

- 10:08:34
- 10:08:35
- 10:08:36
- 10:08:37
- 10:08:38

95th STREET

▸ 10:13:28

▸ 10:13:29

▸ 10:13:30

- 10:19:41
- 10:19:42
- 10:19:43
- 10:19:44
- 10:19:45

FRUIT PATCH, INC.

93rd STREET

▸ 10:26:03
▸ 10:26:04
▸ 10:26:05
▸ 10:26:06
▸ 10:26:07

92nd STREET

▸ 10:28:39

▸ 10:28:40

▸ 10:28:41

▸ 10:28:42

▸ 10:28:43

91st STREET

▸ 10:31:26

▸ 10:31:27

▸ 10:31:28

▸ 10:31:29

▸ 10:31:30

90th STREET

▸ 10:33:58
▸ 10:33:59
▸ 10:34:00
▸ 10:34:01
▸ 10:34:02

MARKET
KOSHER

89th STREET

▶ 10:35:24

▶ 10:35:25

▶ 10:35:26

▶ 10:35:27

▶ 10:35:28

88th STREET

▸ 10:37:06

▸ 10:37:07

▸ 10:37:08

▸ 10:37:09

▸ 10:37:10

87th STREET

▸ 10:38:49

▸ 10:38:50

▸ 10:38:51

▸ 10:38:52

▸ 10:38:53

86th STREET

▸ 10:41:32
▸ 10:41:33
▸ 10:41:34
▸ 10:41:35
▸ 10:41:36